Google Classroom

Easiest Teacher's Guide to Master Google Classroom

Table of Contents

Introduction

Congratulations on downloading *Google Classroom* and thank you for doing so.

Are you a teacher that wants to make your class more organized and effective?

That is what Google Classrooms is going to do!

Classrooms are going to make it to where you are no longer have to give out papers to your class and you are going to be able to monitor the progress of your students as they fulfill the requirements for that class.

Google Classrooms is going to make it to where you are able to save time and make your class run more efficiently as well as make sure that your students are able to do what needs to be done.

Google Classrooms is going to change the way that education is delivered to students and ultimately change education around the world!

The following chapters will discuss how Google is making it to where teachers are going to be able to reach out to students in numerous ways. Google classroom is going to be a way that teachers, students, and parents are all going to be on the same page and it is less likely that a student will lose his homework.

You are going to see that using Google Classroom is going to make it to where as a teacher, you are not going to have to deal with a lot of the headaches that you deal with when having to print out all the assignments that your students need thanks to the fact that it is all online!

here are plenty of books on this subject on the market, thanks again for choosing this one! Every effort was made to ensure it is full of as much useful information as possible, please enjoy!

Chapter one: What is Google Classroom?

The point behind Google Classroom is to offer a platform of blended learning in schools in order to simplify creating assignments and getting the grade out to the students in a paperless way.

Google Classroom was first introduced as something that could be added to G Suite for Education back in 2014 when it was first created and it was released to the public August of that year. June of the following year, it was announced that Google Classroom would have a share button that would enable administrators and developers to continue to engage with Google Classroom.

March of 2017 brought the classroom being opened for personal use for Google users so that they could join classes without needing an education account. April also made it possible for Google users on personal accounts to be able to create and teach classes as they see fit.

Google Classroom took Google Drive and added it to the classroom so that assignments could be created and sent out to the students. Google docs and slides and sheets are used for writing and Gmail is used for communicating back and forth. Finally, the calendar is going to be used to schedule assignments so that students can see what is coming up without having to write it down and lose the paper that they used to write it down on.

Students are going to be invited to classes through the database that is created by the school by using a private code or by being imported through the school's domain. Every class that is made will have a folder that is going to have its own path to that classes drive where students can turn their work in to be graded.

Teachers are going to be able to monitor each student's progress and return work after it has been graded. The teacher can comment on homework so that the students know what they did wrong so that they can improve. Teachers are also going to be able to create class announcements which students will have the ability to comment on.

Google has made claims that Google classroom is not going to show ads if used as part of G Suite for Education due to the fact it is not going to be collecting data for advertising purposes.

Chapter two: Google Classroom Assignments

Any assignment that is created for Google Classroom is going to be stored and graded on the productivity applications that Google offers so that the teacher and student or a group of students can work together.

Rather than sharing documents that are on the Google Drive of the student, the files are going to be hosted by the drive of the student and then submitted to the teacher for grading. A teacher is going to have the option of choosing a file to use as a template in order to allow the students to copy it and make it their own before turning it in rather than the students being allowed to copy or edit the exact same document.

Students are also going to be able to choose if they want to add extra documents to their drive for that particular assignment or not.

Chapter three: Google Classroom Grading

There are several different grading schemes that you are going to be able to choose from as the teacher. You can either attach files for the assignments that the students need to complete so the entire class has access to that attachment. Or, each student can get an individual copy of the assignment.

A student will take files and create them so that they can attach them to the assignment in the event that the teacher did not give them a copy that they could use for their assignment.

As the teacher, you are going to have the ability to monitor the progress that every student is making on their assignment as well as having the option to make comments and edit their assignments.

The assignments that are turned in and graded will be sent back to the student with comments from the teacher so that things can be revised and turned back in done correctly. After the assignment is completely graded, the assignment can only be edited by the teacher unless the teacher sends the document back to the student.

Chapter four: Communicating with Google Classroom

Teachers are going to have the option of posting announcements in a class stream which will then be able to be commented on by the students so that the student and the teacher can communicate about any questions that may arise for that particular assignment.

A student is going to have the option of posting in the class stream but it is not going to be made high priority by Google Classroom because it is not posted by the teacher. Various media types can be used for announcements such as videos from YouTube or files that are located in Google Drive.

Gmail is also going to give teachers and students the option to communicate inside of the interface for Google Classroom.

Students and teachers alike are going to have the ability to access their classroom on the computer or through applications that are made available on mobile devices that use iOS or Android operating systems.

Chapter five: The Time Cost of Using Google Classroom

In order to add a student to a class, the students are going to be given a code from their teacher that is going to get them into the private group specific for that class. The teacher is going to manage several different classes and will be able to reuse the announcements, questions, and assignments that they have used in other classes.

Posts can also be shared across multiple classes and even saved so that they can be used for future classes.

The work, questions, grades, comments, and anything else that is placed in the classroom is going to be sorted so that the teacher will know what is needing to be reviewed. Therefore, saving paper and the teacher is not going to be searching for lost assignments or looking for what they are needed to deal with at that moment.

Chapter six: Archiving Courses

As the class instructor, you are going to be able to archive the course whenever the semester or year ends that way you can use it for a different year.

After a class has been archived, it is going to be taken down from the homepage and moved into the folder where the archived classes are going to be so that the teacher is able to continue to keep that class organized.

Students and teachers are still going to be able to view what is inside of an archived class, however they are not going to be able to modify anything until it has been restored.

Chapter seven: Mobile Applications for Google Classroom

There are mobile applications for Google Classroom that were first introduced in January of 2015. You are going to be able to download these applications on any device that uses iOS or Android operating systems.

These apps make it possible for students and teachers to take photos and turn them in with the assignment as well as share files that are located in other applications and even make it to where you can access the classroom offline if needed.

Chapter eight: The Privacy of Google Classrooms

Google Classrooms are going to have different privacy than other Google services. Since Google Classroom is part of the Education suite that is offered by Google, there are not going to be any advertisements that are shown.

Whenever in the interface, the students and other staff are not going to get their data scanned or used for any advertising purposes.

In fact, data is not going to be collected off of anything from Google Classrooms in order to protect the privacy of the school and its students and staff.

Chapter nine: The Reception of Google Classrooms

The eLearningIndustry made a review of Google Classroom after they tested it. In their review, they highlighted that there are both positive and negative aspects to Google Classroom.

One of the strengths that Google Classroom has is that it is easy to use, uses Google Drive in an effective way that makes it easy for teachers to share assignments, it is accessible on almost any device, and it is paperless. Another advantage is that it offers immediate feedback from the teacher to the students.

Some of the disadvantages are that there is a heavy integration process with the Google apps and service that are limited and do not have any support to go with them when it comes to external files or services. There is the lack of automated quizzes and tests, no discussion forms or live chats that can be used for feedback and helping students with their assignments.

Google is always being criticized for allegedly data mining the history and searches from students accounts in order to use it for advertising purposes. However, in April of 2014, it was announced that the emails of students would no longer be scanned in order to fix the privacy concerns of parents and other Google members.

It was written by TechCrunch that the ads are not included in the educational program data and information that is pulled from their users.

Chapter ten: Your Google Classroom

It is only going to take a few minutes to create a new class or post resources or even set permissions for your students. After you have done this you are going to be able to invite students directly to the class or by sending them a code.

Creating classes

1. On a computer, you are going to go to classroom.Google.com
2. Select the plus sign then choose the create class button.
3. You will then enter the name of the class.
4. Enter in text like grade level and what time the class is.
5. Also put a subject line in
6. Select create.

Your class is going to automatically be given a code that is going to be used to invite students. You have the option of changing the themes and putting a photo for the class. Should you not need the class anymore you can archive it.

Accepting provisioned classes

Whoever manages the classroom is going to be able to create classes for their teachers as well as adding students to them. Any classes that are made by the administrator are going to be placed in a provisioned state. As the teacher you will need to sign in and accept the invitation to the class before it is visible to students.

1. Go to classroom.Google.com
2. Move to the classes card and choose accept.
3. Ensure that the number of students in the class is accurate before choosing accept.

Changing the theme

Once you have created the class, you have the option of changing the image and colors of the class. Only teachers have the ability to change the theme.

1. Sign into classroom.Google.com
2. Move to the bottom of the class image and choose the select theme button.
3. Pick one of the following options
   a. Pick a pattern.
   b. Choose an image from the gallery.

Uploading your own image

1. Open your class and pick upload photo.
2. Pick one of these options
   a. Move a picture over to the middle of the screen.
   b. Select a photo from your computer.

Editing class information

1. Enter classroom.Google.com into your URL
2. Move to the class card and select the three little dots. A menu will pop up which will give you the option of editing the class.
3. Enter the new information and hit save.

Displaying a profile picture

You have the ability to place a photo next to the name of your class. Automatically your classroom is going to use your Google account photo so you will want to make sure that you are using an appropriate picture.

Problems creating classes

In the event that you are using a G Suite Education account and find that you are unable to add classes, then the administrator of the suite is going to need to verify that you are a teacher in their domain. So, make sure that you are contacting your administrator for any help that you may need.

Note: should you be using a personal Google account, then you are going to be limited on how many classes you are going to be able to create.

Adding a class to a resource page

Once a class has been created, you are going to have the ability to add class information and resources to your class in the about page. You are going to be able to post materials and instructions for your class so that they can know how you grade, what to expect throughout the year, so on so forth. This information can be added or removed at any point in time.

Adding class information

1. Go to the website classroom.Google.com
2. Move to the about section. The name of the class is going to automatically be entered there.
3. You can add in a description or a location for the class. But, if you leave these fields blank, they are not going to appear in what the students see for your class.
4. Save.

Resource materials

1. Under the class information section you will see a button that says add class materials and a title can be entered there.
2. You will have the option of adding in multiple resources under one title or adding them in separately under specific names.
    a. In order to attach a file, click on the appropriate icon.
    b. Find the item that you are wanting to attach and click add. Should you decide that you do not need that item anymore just click on remove.
    c. Post.

Your email address and a link to the folder where the attachment is located will be automatically included with every item that is added to the resource page. This cannot be changed.

Editing your about page

1. Go to the classroom web page.
2. Move to the about section.
3. Click on the three dots and select the edit button.
4. Make any changes that you see fit and then save them.

Joining classes by invitation

You can not only create your own class, but you can be invited to classes so that you can become a co teacher in a class. Co teachers are going to have the option of performing all of the teacher tasks once they have joined that class.

Accepting an invitation

1. Go to the classroom web page.
2. Accept the invitation or decline it if you do not want to be a co teacher.
3. You can also select the invitation through the email that you get.

Note: when a student declines the invitation to become a co teacher, they are not going to be removed from the class.

Inviting teachers to a class

Teachers can be invited to co teach a class or to help coordinate class activities. In using Google groups, groups of teachers can be invited at the same time.

Inviting co teachers or groups of co teachers

You are not going to have to be the owner of the group but you are going to need to be a member of the group in order to be invited others to the group.

1. Log into your classroom.
2. Go to the class that you are wanting to add co teachers to.
3. Move to the about section.
4. Click on the invite teachers button.
5. Individual teachers or groups of teachers can be entered by entering the group email or the teacher's email.
6. Click on the teacher or group and select add.
7. You can invite as many teachers or groups as you want by repeating the same steps.
8. Select invite.

Note: your class is going to be updated to show those who have been invited. An email is going to be received by the teacher so that they can join the class by clicking on the join class card.

Permissions for co teachers

These permissions are going to need to be made aware of by all of the teachers in a class.

- Only the main teacher has the ability to delete the class.
- Co teachers who join a class can access the Google Drive folder.
- Primary teachers cannot withdraw or be removed from their own class.
- Teachers cannot be muted.
- The primary teacher is the owner of the Google Drive folder.

Class size

G Suite accounts

If you are using a G suite account then you are going to be able to have up to twenty teachers and a thousand members of both teachers and students

Note: Classrooms are going to use groups for the students and teachers that are using the education suite accounts. Every person is only going to be allowed in a certain number of groups.

Personal accounts

When using a personal account there are going to be other limits put on activities such as creating or inviting people.

Inviting students

Students are going to have to be enrolled in your class through an invitation or a code that is given to them by you. If you are using Google groups you can invite an entire group of students at the same time.

Inviting students or groups of students

You are not going to have to own the group to invite students, you just have to be a member of it.

1. Go to the classroom website.
2. Go to the class you are wanting to invite people to.
3. Move to students and then click on invite students.
4. You are going to be able to invite individual students or groups of students by entering their email address.
5. When looking at the search results, you are going to click on the student or the group of students before hitting add.
6. Invite more students by repeating steps four and five.
7. Select invite..

Note: the class will be updated once students select the join button on their class card

Giving out the class code

1. Log into your Google classroom.
2. Go to students and the code will be located to the left under class code.
3. Select copy.
4. Send the code to the students in an email or write it out on the board in your class whenever your students are setting up their accounts.
5. The students should follow these instructions

a. Sign in to the classroom website.
b. Go to join class on the home screen.
c. Enter the code and then select join.

Inviting students not in the school domain

As long as the school administrator allows the permission to be turned on so that you can invite students to your class that are not in your school's domain

Resetting or disabling the class code

Should a student or students have a problem with your class code you can either reset it or disable it.

1. Go to your classroom.
2. Move to the students tab where the code is located.
3. Select the code and choose reset or disable.
4. If you want to enable a code that has been disabled just click on enable.

Removing a student

Whenever a student is taken out of a class their work is going to stay in their folder. You can delete their work and posts if you need to.

1. Go to Google Classrom.
2. Move to the student section.
3. Click on the box that appears next to the name of the student that needs to be removed.
4. Go to the top of the page and click on actions and then remove.
5. Make sure to hit confirm before removing the students.

Removing a teacher

The only person who can remove teachers from classes is the primary teacher. The primary teacher cannot be removed from their own class.

1. Log into Google Classrooms.
2. Go to the class that you are wanting to modify.
3. Go to the about section.
4. Locate the teacher's name and click on the three dots to open the menu.
5. Select remove from class.
6. Confirm and remove.

Archiving a class

When the semester or school year ends you have the option of archiving the class so you can use the material later. In archiving a class it is going to be removed so you no longer see it in an effort to keep your other classes organized.

Note: whenever a class becomes archived it will no longer show up on a students feed.

After a class has been archived it cannot be modified until it is restored.

1. Go to Google classroom
2. Move to the class card and select archive
3. Confirm to complete the process

Looking at an archived class

1. Go to your Google Classroom.
2. Select the menu and move to archived classes.

3. Select which class it is that you are wanting to look at.

Restoring an archived class

A class can be restored after it has been archived, all you are going to need to do is move to the class card so that you can update your class.

1. Log into Google Classroom.
2. Go to the archived classes menu.
3. Select the three dots and go to the restore option.
4. Click restore to confirm that you want the class to be restored.

Deleting a class that has been archived

When you permanently delete a class, it has to be archived first. Classes cannot be deleted unless they have been archived.

1. Move to the Google classroom website.
2. Select archived classes.
3. On the class card, click delete
4. Confirm your deletion.

Note: you cannot undo the deleting of a class. Once you have clicked the delete button you are not going to have access to that class any longer or anything that is going to be posted in it. The only thing that you will have access to is the files for that class that are located on the drive.

Tracking assignments and events

You will have the ability to track the questions and assignments that your class does on a calender. When a class is created in

Google Classroom, your students are going to see the class calender in your classroom as well as on their Google calender.

On the classroom calender, the students are going to see what assignments are due. On their Google calender, they will see the events that you add like test dates, field trips so on and so forth.

If there are no calenders see for your classes, then your administrator may have turned the calender permissions off for your account.

Viewing assignment due dates

Whenever an assignment is created, it will automatically add the due date to the class calender. Your students are going to be able tos ee these assignments in the classroom calender or their Google calender.

1. Log into Google Classroom.
2. Go to the menu located at the top of the page.
3. Select calender.
4. Pick an assignment or question and open it.
5. You can view past and future work by clicking the next button.
6. You can see the assignments for every class that you manage by selecting all classes. In order to see the assignments for a single class click on all classes and select which class you want to see.

Adding events to Google Calender

In order to track events like tests you will add them to your Google calender. All a student is going to have to do is open the calender and they will be able to see the events.

1. Go to Google classroom.
2. Select the class you want to view.
3. Go to the about section.
4. Next to the calender option, choose open in Google calender.

See posts and sharing permissions

Students are allowed to post messages in the class stream as well as comment on anything the teacher or their classmates may post. You are going to be able to control what the students post by setting up permissions for specific students or the entire class. You are also able to delete posts made by students.

Setting permissions for a class

1. Find the class that you are wanting to set the permissions for.
2. Go to the students section.
3. Choose a permission level from the post and comment list.
   a. Students are allowed to post and comment: this is going to be the default setting. Students are going to be able to share messages to the class stream and comment on anything that is posted in the class.
   b. Students can only comment: the students are not going to be allowed to share messages.
   c. Only teacher can post or comment: this is essentially muting all the students so that they cannot do anything but look at what you post.

Muting a student

When a student is muted, they are not going to be able to comment or post on the class stream. Other students are not going to see anything in the stream to show them that they have been muted. They are just not going to have the option of posting.

Muting students on the student page

1. Go to the class where the students are.
2. Go to the student tab.
3. Select the box next to the student that you want to mute.
4. Select actions and then mute.
5. Confirm the muting of the student.

Mute a student on their post or comment

1. Find the class where the student is.
2. Find where they have posted or commented.
3. Click on more and select mute "student's name".
4. Confirm the muting.
5. You can delete the comment by
   a. Clicking on the three dots and hitting delete
   b. Click on delete again

Unmuting a student

When unmuting a student, they are going to be able to post and comment on things in the class stream.

Unmute from the student page

1. Go to the students page.

2. Move to the students section.
3. Click on which students you want to unmute.
4. Go to actions and unmute.
5. Confirm and unmute once more.

Unmute from a post

1. Find the class the student is in.
2. Find where they have commented or messaged on something.
3. Click the three dots and select unmute "student name".
4. Confirm to unmute a student.

Delete a post or comment made by a student

1. Find the class you want to modify.
2. Find the post or comment and click on more.
3. Go to delete and then confirm.

Seeing what has been deleted

1. Go to the class where there are deleted comments or posts
2. Under the stream option click on show
3. In order to hide them, click hide and they will be hidden.

Chapter eleven: Gurdians and Google Classroom

If you are the guardian of a student who is using Google Classrooms, you are going to be able to receive summaries about your student that have school accounts.

These emails are going to give you a summary about the progress that your student is making in their class. You will have the option to choose how frequently you get the emails or you can unsubscribe from them at any time that you need to.

The guardian emails are going to include:

- Missing work: whenever work is late and has not been turned in.
- Upcoming work: work that is due that day or the next. This is only going to come on daily emails. If you are getting weekly emails, then you will get the work for that week.
- Class activity: anything that is posted by the teacher so that you can keep up making sure your student is doing their work.

Removing yourself as guardian

If at any point in time you want to remove yourself as the guardian of a student, you may do so. It is going to be easiest if you have a Google account.

1. Go to the bottom of an email summary and select settings
2. Find the students name and select the trashcan

However, if you do not have a Google account you will

1. Go an email summary and select unsubscribe.
2. You will have to click it again to make sure that you are aware you are permanently deleting yourself as guardian.

If you remove yourself as a guardian, the student is going to get an email allowing them to know.

Chapter twelve: Email Summaries

Email summaries are going to let you keep up to date about what is going on in your students class. Before you are able to get summaries, you need to first have a Google account due to the fact that it makes things a lot easier on you in the long run.

Creating a Google account

In order to manage your email summaries, you will need to get a free Google account. You are not going to need to have a Google email address to create the account, you are going to be able to use any email that you access most often.

1. Inside of the email program that you use, go to the bottom of an email summary and select the settings button.
2. When it goes to the email settings page, you will create a new account
3. From there you are going to fill out the information that is requested and submit it, then the email settings page is going to open.

Receive email summaries

As the parent or guardian of a student, you are going to be enabled to recieve and accept an email invitation that is going to mean that you can recieve email summaries on your student. The only people who are going to be allowed to send out these invitations are the teachers or the administrators of the school.

Once the invitation has been sent, you are going to have a hundred and twenty days to accept the invitation or else it is going to expire.

1. The administrator or the teacher is going to send you an email invitation for a particular student. This email can be sent to any email that you want it sent to.
2. Once you get the invitation, you will go to the email and open it.
3. Next you will click accept. In the event that you are not the guardian of a student you are going to select not the guardian option.

After you have accepted the invitation, the person who invited you as well as the student is going to get an email alerting them that you have accept it and are now going to be getting email updates.

Whenever an email summary won't be sent

There are times that you are not going to get an email update and those times are going to be:

- When there is no activity to be reported for that period of time.
- Your student's teacher has notifications off for that class.
- You have chosen not to recieve summaries
- You are not connected to a student in that classroom.

Managing email summary settings

In order to manage email summaries you are going to need a Google account as we described earlier. Having a Google account is going to allow you to:

- View any student that is connected to your account
- Set up the frequency in which you get emails
- Update your location

Ito manage your email settings you will

1. Create a Google account if you have not already.
2. Sign into that account.
3. Move to your email and go to the bottom of your summary and click on settings.
4. Sign into the email settings page.
5. Enter your account email and select the next button.
6. Enter your password and sign into your account.
7. If you move to the frequency button you can change how frequently you recieve emails, if you do not want any emails, then select the no summaries option.
8. Under the time zone setting you can choose which time zone you reside in.
9. To look and see what email summaries you are going to recieve you will look under the Google classroom email summaries tab.

Unsubscribing from summaries

Email summaries can be unsubscribed from at any time. Keep your Google account so that you can reconnect with your student if you want to.

1. Once again, if you have not already created a Google account, you are going to want to.
2. Go to the bottom of your email and select unsubscribe.

Note: if you are a guardian, this is going to remove you from your students account as guardian if you are not using a free Google account.

Chapter thirteen: Extending Your Classroom

Getting the Classroom application

Whether you are a student or a teacher, you will have the option of installing the Classroom app on Android, Chrome, or App devices. This app is not currently available on Windows devices. If you are using a desktop, you will go to the Classroom website and log in.

After getting the app, you will sign in either as a teacher or as a student. As a teacher you are going to be able to manage your classroom from wherever you are.

Downloading the app

Android

1. Go to Google Play.
2. Locate the Google Classroom app and download.

iOS

The Google classroom app can be downloaded on an iPhone or iPad.

1. Go to your app store.
2. Install the Google Classroom app.

ChromeOS

The app is going to be like a bookmark on the internet. You can also go to the Chrome Web Store and download it from there.

Managed devices

In the event that your students school uses devices that are managed, the student may not have the option of installing the app themselves.

Should you be a teacher at a school that uses managed devices, you are going to have Google play for education access.

If you can get access from your admin console, you can then get the app sent out to your students so they can download it. You will also have the ability to send Google Drive and doc apps.

If you cannot get access, then you need to contact your school's administrator.

Chapter fourteen: Installing the Chrome Extension for Google Classroom

Both teachers and students that are using a chrome browser to access Google Classroom, you can share pages with the "share to classroom chrome extension". As a teacher, you can also use the extension to post announcements or assignments.

Who has the ability to install the extension

- Administrators: any administrator will be able to install the extension for any member that works for them.this is going to make it to where there is not as much time having to trouble shoot requests and makes sure that both teachers and students can instantly get started with the extension.
- Students: a teacher can post installation instructions in their class which enables the student to install the extension.
- Teachers: will get the ability to install the extension from their admin.

Admin install instructions

You will only be able to use G Suite for Education to preinstall the extension for those who fall under them.

1. Sign into your admin console.
2. Go to device management.
3. Move on to chrome management and then user settings.
4. Choose which unit you want to modify the settings for. Should you decide to change the settings for everyone, you need to select the top level unit or one of the child units.

5. Find the apps and extensions section which is going to be next to the force installed apps and extensions. You are going to need to choose the manage force installed apps.
6. Move on to the web store for chrome and search for share to classroom.
7. Now go to the extension and select add then save.

Teacher install instructions

1. First you are going to go to g.co/sharetoclassroom
2. Now you will select add to chrome.
3. Then click on add extension. You should see the share to classroom button at the top right of your address bar.
4. When you share to classroom an extension is going to be opened. Note: you are going to need to be signed into chrome in order to use the extension.

Posting installation instructions for your students

1. Select this link: https://classroom.Google.com/share?url=https%3A%2F%2Fg.co%2Fsharetoclassroom&body=Open%20the%20following%20link%20to%20install%20the%20Share%20to%20Classroom%20Chrome%20extension&title=Install%20the%20Share%20to%20Classroom%20Chrome%20extension
2. Pick which class you want to share the link to.
3. Select what type of post by clicking on choose action.
4. Select an option
   a. Make an announcement
   b. Create assignment
   c. Ask question
5. Pick the go button. A post is going to be opened with the instructions on how to add the attachment.

6. Select an option that will go with the instructions that you post.
   a. Select post if you are posting an announcement
   b. Click assign if you are posting an assignment
   c. And pick ask if you are asking a question
7. You can pick the view button in order to see what is being posted in the class stream.

Installation instructions for students

You are going to install the extension from the instructions that your teacher posted to your class stream.

1. Sign into your classroom with the Google account you created.
2. Go to your class.
3. Find the post that says share to classroom – chrome web store.
4. Add to chrome.
5. Add the extension. A share to classroom icon will appear at the top right of your screen next to your address bar.
6. Select this icon and you are going to open the extension. Make sure that you are signed into chrome before you do this.

Chapter fifteen: Using Screen Reader with Classroom

If a teacher or a student is blind or has low vision you are going to be able to use a screen reader on the computer or mobile device that is going to make it easier for them to see what is on the screen.

Web

Classroom can be accessed through the internet using a screen reader. You have the option of using any browser that you want and you are going to have to follow the instructions set forth by that browser on how to set up the screen reader. If you are using a Mac you can use voice over with your screen reader.

Mobile

Android

The Android Classroom app is going to work with the talkback application that is going to be preinstalled with the screen reader. Talkback uses spoken feedback for its interaction.

iOS

Just like Android uses talkback, iOS is going to use voiceover.

Chapter sixteen: Google Classroom API

Technology companies are working with schools to use Classroom API in order to build the tools needed to interact with the G suite and classroom so that they work better to meet the needs of the teacher and their students. API is a Google developer API which means that any non Google service is going to be able to benefit from the tools and infrastructure offered by Google.

In order to use the classroom API, the developer is going to need to agree to the API terms of service. Other applications are not going to be able to use data collected from Google Classroom for any advertising purposes.

Who can use classroom API

Any third party developer or administrator is going to be able to use Classroom API. Students and teachers are going to have the option to authorize third party applications so that they can use API as well.

What can you do with API

When using API you will have the ability to program things that typical students and teachers will use through the classroom UI. For example, you will have the option of synchronizing your student information so that you can see the classes that are being taught in that domain and then manage the classwork that is required for that particular class.

If a non Google service is using the API to integrate features that will be used with classroom, they may be able to do things such as allow the teacher to copy and reuse things that they used in their classroom so that they do not have to go back and recreate everything. Applications are also going to be able to modify the work in the classroom as well as add material, turn in work, and send back grades.

Applications and classroom data

Apps and services have access to the data that comes from a Google Classroom. However, apps are going to need to get authorization from the user before it uses data. App will typically ask for specific pieces of information to collect. As the user, you can agree to share the data or not. When authorizing the app to use data it is going to use Oauth which is a common standard to be used over the internet for authenitcating the approval to collect data.

G Suite for Education Admins

If you are an administrator in G Suite then you are going to be allowed to control just how much data you allow to be shared inside of your domain. From the admin console, you will specify who you want to authorize the services so that data can be accessed. You also have the ability to configure the access that is given by the organizational unit.

Also inside of the admin console you will have the option of looking at the services that are going to be granted access to an account in your domain so that you can remove privileges if needed.

Classroom API for users

There are particular tasks that can be done by Classroom API depending on what role the user occupies. Just like with the classroom UI, the user is going to be an administrator, teacher, or student. The teachers and students are going to be able to approve of any third party applications that need to be approved as well as report abuse inside of the classroom.

So, what can API do for you?

Student:

- Look at the details of the course and the teacher of that course.

Teacher:

- Create and modify classes.
- Set grades.
- Create assignments.
- Return work.
- View and modify class roster.

Administrator:

- Create and modify classes in G Suite.
- View work being done in classes.
- Add or remove students and staff from domain.

Chapter seventeen: Students and Their Google Classroom

You will sign into your classroom from your G Suite account or your personal Google account. Once you have signed in, you are going to be able to update the profile picture that is being used with your classroom profile or you can manage your password and settings for your Google account.

Signing into a Google classroom

You can use a G Suite for Education account or you can use a personal Google account.

Signing in

1. Go to classroom.Google.com and click on sign in
2. Enter your log in information before clicking on next.

Keep in mind that your Suite username is going to use a .edu email while your personal account will use a .com email.

3. Enter your password before signing in.
4. Should there be a welcome message, you are going to want to read it and then accept the terms and conditions.
5. If you are using a G Suite account, select that you are a student
6. Choose the get started button

Trouble signing in

If you are having this problem, there are several things that you may be able to do. Let's look at each situation and solution for that problem.

1. Your service is disabled by the admin.

This means that the classroom has not been activated for the account that you are using. What you need to do is contact your teacher or the school administrator to have them activate the classroom for you.

2. The classroom is only available for Education users only.

This means that you have tried to use a personal account instead of a school account. What you are going to have to do is go to your web browser and sign in with your education account. If you are using the mobile app you are going to need to use a different account to sing in with your education account.

Another issue could mean that your school is not using the G Suite for Education. If this happens, then your school needs to sign up for G Suite before Classrooms can be accessed.

3. Your administrator hasn't activated Classroom.

To use this classroom you need to contact your school's IT or G Suite Admin to activate the classroom. Your school is not using G Suite and to fix this issue you will need your school to sign up for G Suite.

Accessing classroom

By going to the menu, you can access other parts of Google Classrooms.

- Settings: you can change your passwords, notifications, and profile picture.
- Classes: you can look at all your classes that are using Google Classrooms.

- Work: see all of the assignments and posts associated with the assignment.
- Calendar: look at assignment due dates, test days, so on and so forth.

Managing classes

You are either going to get an email to join a class or get an access code from your teacher. Once you have joined you are going to see the class stream where you are going to be able to locate class resources.

Joining a class

In order to get into the Google Classroom that your teacher creates, you are going to need to sign into your classroom account and then join your teacher's class. There are two different ways to join a class as we have discussed throughout this book.

Your teacher can give you a code, you will use this code to add yourself to the class. Or, you are going to get an invitation in your email and you will need to select join that appears on the class card.

If you get deleted from the class or you lose or forget the class code, you can ask your teacher to give you a new code.

Note: you are only going to need to enroll once, once you have enrolled, there is not going to be any need for you to reuse the code.

Using a code to join the class

1. Go to Google Classrooms.

2. Go to the top and click the plus sign where it says join class.
3. In the box insert the class code that was given to you by the teacher before hitting join.

Accepting an invitation

1. Go to the Google Classroom website.
2. Go to the class stream and select join.

Note: the teacher is the only person who can change the image for the class, but you can change the profile picture for your classroom.

Withdrawing from a class

When you no longer need to be enrolled in a class, you can remove the class so your current classes remain organized. Teachers may archive their class but not all of them will do this. Therefore, you can withdraw from the class when you sign into Classrooms. But, you are still going to have access to your files from that class.

1. Go to Google classroom.
2. Move to the class card and select the more menu before clicking unenroll.
3. Confirm your unenrollment.

Viewing archived classes

When a teacher archives a class it is going to be moved to a new area in your classroom account. After the class is archived, you can still view the class and all of its material but you cannot submit or delete any of the material.

Once the class has been restored, you will be able to interact with it like you were able to before it was archived. However, if it gets deleted, your class is going to be permanently deleted.

Note: archived or deleted classes will still allow you to see the class files located on Google drive.

1. Go to Google Classrooms.
2. Go to the menu and choose archived classes.
3. Click on the class that you are wanting to look at.

Note: a teacher is the only person who can delete a class, if you want to leave the class you will need to unenroll from the class.

Viewing your classes resource page

Teachers can add resources for you to to use which are going to store information like the policies for the class, how they grade things, so on and so forth. There is also going to be a link to your teacher's email address and a link to the folder for that class on Google Drive.

1. Go to the about section.
2. Click on the item that you are wanting to view.

Viewing assignments on the calendar

You will be able to track the assignments and questions that have due dates on a class calendar. Therefore, your teacher is going to make an assignment in the class which will automatically be placed on the calendar for both the classroom calendar and the Google calendar. On your class calendar, you are going to see the due dates for assignments as well as any events that are coming up.

Viewing assignments due dates

1. Go to the menu at the top of the page.
2. Choose calendar.
3. Choose which assignment you want to open.
4. Click on next to look at past and future work.
5. Choose all classes to see work for all your Google classes.

Viewing class events

1. Go to your class.
2. Move to the about section.
3. On calender click on open in Google calendar.

Now you can see upcoming tests or field trips.

View work

You are going to be able to view your work on any class card that is located in your stream or you can go to the work tab in your Google classroom.

Upcoming work

Any unfinished or upcoming work that is due for that week will show up on your class card.

1. For every class you are going to see the upcoming work work and the due date that goes along with that assignment.
2. Click on the title to see all the instructions.

Work in the class stream

1. Go to your class.

2. Select the title for any instructions or feedback that may be attached to it.
3. In order to add a comment click on the add class comment or number class comment located at the top of the page.
4. Sending your teacher a private comment will be done by clicking on add private comment.

Viewing work on work page

1. Go to the menu and then go to work.
2. Select the title you want to look at.
3. Click add class comment to comment on something.
4. Click add private comment to send a private comment to your teacher.
5. Any work that you have already submitted can viewed by clicking on the done button at the top of the page. If the teacher has already graded the work, then there is going to be a grade with that assignment.

Answering questions

Teachers are going to be able post questions in their classes stream and the student is going to have the option of answering them. The questions are going to be able to contain attachments to files or videos.

Answering short answer questions

1. Pick the class you have a question to answer in. The question is going to appear in your stream.
2. If an attachment is there, then you will need to click on it and review it before submitting your answer.
3. Enter your answer and hit the submit button. You are going to need to hit confirm before your answer is sent.

The submit button is not going to be visible if you have not put an answer in.

4. You can send comments or private comments if you need to to get clarification on your question.

Note: your teacher may make it to where you can see how your classmates answered the question once you have submitted your answer.

Multiple choice questions

1. Go to the class.
2. Look at any attachments that may be there.
3. Pick which answer you think is suitable for the question and click submit.

Viewing and replying to answers by classmates

For the short answer questions, your teacher may make it to where you can see and even reply to the answers that your classmates submitted after you submit your answer. If your teacher does not turn this permission on, then you are not going to have this option. But, if you do, you can click on the see classmates answers on your question once you have submitted your answer.

1. Go to your class.
2. Go to the see classmate answers on the question.
3. Reply to any classmates answer by hitting reply and then posting that reply.

Editing your answer

For the short answer questions you may be able to edit your answer once you have submitted it. But, this is only going to work if your teacher allows for that permission to be turned on.

1. Go to your class.
2. Find the question and select the edit button.
3. Make your changes and hit submit once again.

Viewing returned work

A teacher can return any work that they want you to look at again and you are going to be able to view it on the work page or in your class stream. The work may not be graded when it is returned and this is going to be done so that you can edit the assignment and then turn it back in.

Viewing returned work on the work page

1. Go to the menu and select the work tab.
2. Select done to see what has already been submitted and graded. If there is any work that has been graded, then it is going to have a grade next to it.
3. You can sort your work out by class by going to the all classes filter and choosing a class to view.

View work in class stream

1. Go to the class that you want to view.
2. Select work and if you see a grade, then that assignment has been graded.

Writing notes on your work

There are tools in the Google classroom that make it to where you can add drawing and writing tools on your assignments. Words can be underlined, highlighted, shapes drawn, and notes left. You also have the option of drawing and writing on Adobe files, PDF files, Google Docs, and Microsoft Office documents.

Note: these tools are only going to be available when using the app on Android or Apple iOS.

1. Go to the classroom icon on your browser.
2. Go to your class and choose your assignment.
3. Look at the file if there is one attached.
4. If you need to create a new PDF you will open a blank file and write out anything that needs to be on that file.
5. Notes can be made with the drawing and writing tools.
6. Click the save icon to save your notes.

Note: you have to make sure that you are saving your work because the changes are not going to be saved automatically. If you leave the screen then you are going to lose your work.

7. You can open your work in Google drive by opening a new tab.

Saving notes

Should the original file be an image or a PDF file, the editing the file is going to overwrite the original file.

If the file is an office document or a Google docs file, the file you edit will be saved as a PDF.

Adding web pages to your assignments

Should you see the share to classroom button on a page, you will be able to use the button to post the web page on the assignment in your classroom. The share to classroom icon is going to usually placed next to social media icons.

Should a page not have this icon, then you can still submit the web page by using the URL.

1. Click the share to classroom icon.
2. Sign into your classroom.
3. Pick which class you want to share the URL on. You have to make sure that there is an upcoming assignment in that class.
4. Pick the assignment you want it attached to.
5. Hit the go button.
6. Attach the link.
7. View your assignment.

Connecting with your class

In order to connect with your classmates is to post on the class stream. You will also be able to see class announcments and take part in class discussions. If you need help from your teacher, you can email them directly.

Posting to the class stream

You can share things with your class or comment on things that they post in the class stream unless the teacher has removed this permission. All of the posts and comments made by any student is going to be visible to the entire class.

Ways to post

- Reply to a comment
- Create a new post
- Add a comment to someone else's post
- Add a comment to any post made by the teacher

Creating a post

1. Go to the class.
2. Move to the bottom and click the plus button then select create post.
3. In the box you will type in your message.
4. You can attach files if you need to.
5. If you are not wanting to post then hit the button that says cancel.
6. Post your comment.

Adding a comment to a post

1. Go to the class.
2. Find the post and click on the add class comment which is located on the post.
3. Enter your comment and post.
4. If you do not want to post your comment, then hit the cancel button.

Replying to a comment

1. Find your class in Google Classrooms.
2. Hover over any comment that you want to reply to and click on the reply button. The person that you are replying to is going to be mentioned automatically.
3. Put your comment in the box and post

Deleting posts and comments

When a post is deleted, all the comments will be deleted along with it. You are not going to be able to undo this action.

1. Go to your class
2. Find the post or comment and click on the more button.
3. Then go to delete and make sure you confirm it so that you can get rid of it.

Mentioning classmates in posts

Should you want to mention someone in a post in your classroom you can use the plus button or the at symbol along with that person's email. Both your classmates or teacher can be mentioned in a post or comment or even comment replies so that you can add them to the discussion or so that they can see what you wrote.

Whenever someone is mentioned they are going to get emails and you are going to recieve emails too, but only if the notifications are on for their account settings.

The plus sign or the at symbol is only going to work when posting in the class stream.

+ mentions

1. Go to that class.
2. Insert your message in the comment box. Or your post in the new post box on the main screen.
3. Insert your mention before typing the person's name and choosing the name from the autocomplete list that appears.

4. If you want to pick a different name, go down the list until you find that person and then select enter.
5. Post your comment or post.

Note: if the name that you want is not appearing, then you are going to need to enter the entire email address for that person.

Viewing comments

Go to your gmail to see any notifications about comments that are posted in the class stream.

Replying to comments

You can reply to comments or posts in the class stream by going to that post or comment and entering in your own comment.

Sending emails

When using classroom from personal Google accounts your administrator may make it to where your contact sharing has been disabled which will make it to where you will not see the email button next to the names of your teacher or classmates.

Emailing a teacher

1. Go to the class of the teacher that you are wanting to email.
2. Move to the about section.
3. Under the teacher's name to the left is going to be an email button. Click on it and a new email box will appear on your screen.
4. Type in your email and hit send.

Emailing students

1. Go to the class that you share with that student.
2. Go to the classmates tab.
3. Find the name of the student and click on the three dot menu then choose email classmate. A message box is going to be opened.
4. Write out your message and send it.

Sharing a web page with a teacher

If you are using the chrome browser, then you will have the option of sharing a web page from the computer to the teacher's computer via the classroom chrome extension. This extension allows your teacher to send web pages back to you.

Sharing a web page with your teacher

The extension must be enabled on your computer as well as your teacher's computer so that you can share with each other. If you do not have the extension or are not sure if you do, then ask your teacher about it.

1. In the browser, go to the address bar and locate the share to classroom button.
2. Sign into your classroom account.
3. Find the name of your teacher's class and click on it.

Note: should you not have any classes joined, you will need to join an open class.

4. Select the push to teacher button, you are going to instantly be sending a message to your teacher with the web page you are wanting to share.

View recently shared pages

1. Go to the address back and click on the share to classroom icon.
2. Find the name of your teacher's class.
3. Go to the websites that you want to view.
   a. Received from teacher: these are web pages that your teacher sent you
   b. Pushed to teacher: these are the web pages that you sent your teacher

The web pages are going to automatically update whenever you send something to your teacher these pages are going to vanish after a certain period of time. You are not going to be able to remove these pages yourself.

Filtering your class stream

In the class stream you can see that the posts are going to be arranged by the time that they are posted. The most recent post is always going to appear at the top of the stream. If at any time your teacher creates topics, you are going to be able to filter your stream by these topics. If there are no topics created, then you will not be able to do this.

1. Select the class you want to enter.
2. Choose one of the options
   a. Go to a post and click on the topic to filter out for that specific topic.
   b. On the left there is a topics button that you can click and then select which topic you are wanting to view on your stream.

Chapter eighteen: The Drawing and Writing Tool

Choosing a tool

These tools can be located at the bottom of the app screen.

- Add text: add in a text note to your file.
- Write: draw or write lines with a writing device. The pressure is going to determine how wide the lines are.
- Erase: a note will be erased.
- Mark: a marker will be used to edit the file.
- Select: a note will be selected to move it or change its size.
- Highlight: images and text will be highlighted.

Changing the color or size

When writing, highlighting, or marking you can change the size ad color of the tool.
1. Pick a tool by tapping on it.
2. Change the color or size by using the up arrow.

Adding text notes

1. Click on the add text button.
2. Move your finger over the file so you create a new text field.
3. Insert your message.
   a. Tap a corner of the box to resize it.
   b. Use two fingers and pinch apart to make the text bigger.
   c. Use two fingers and pinch together to make smaller.

Erasing marks

1. Select the eraser.
2. Tap on a mark to erase it.
3. Double tap the eraser to remove all of the marks that are on the page.

Resizing or moving a note

1. Pick the select tool and tap on the note or image.
2. Use two fingers to pinch together or apart to resize.
3. Drag the note where you want it to be when moving it.

Zooming in and out

Use two fingers and pinch fingers apart to zoom out.

Use two fingers and pinch together to zoom in.

Drag your fingers over the screen to pan across the screen.

Undo or redo

Tap the undo button to cancel the action. Hit it multiple times to undo multiple actions at once.

To redo the action, hit the redo button. Hit it several times to redo the action.

Conclusion

Thank you for making it through to the end of *Google Classroom*, let's hope it was informative and able to provide you with all the tools you need to achieve your goals whatever it may be.

The next step is to decide if Google Classroom is right for your class. You are going to have the ability to keep everything organized and you are not going to be losing things like you might typically do.

As you saw demonstrated in this book, Google Classroom is going to be good for most classes because you are going to be able to communicate with the students and teachers even outside of school. On top of that it is going to be easily accessible and you are going to be saving time in using it.

In the end, as the world of technology and education evolves to meet the needs of those that are using it, you are going to see that Google Classroom is going to be used more and more so that classes are taught more effectively.

Finally, if you found this book useful in any way, a review on Amazon is always appreciated!

Thank you and good luck!

CPSIA information can be obtained
at www.ICGtesting.com
Printed in the USA
LVHW01s0234150618
580860LV00020B/844/P